# THE TENNESSEE WALKING HORSE

By Sara Green

Consultant:
Dr. Emily Leuthner
DVM, MS, DACVIM
Country View Veterinary Service
Oregon, Wisc.

BELLWETHER MEDIA • MINNEAPOLIS, MN

Jump into the cockpit and take flight with Pilot Books. Your journey will take you on high-energy adventures as you learn about all that is wild, weird, fascinating, and fun!

This edition first published in 2012 by Bellwether Media, Inc.

No part of this publication may be reproduced in whole or in part without written permission of the publisher. For information regarding permission, write to Bellwether Media, Inc., Attention: Permissions Department, 5357 Penn Avenue South, Minneapolis, MN 55419.

Library of Congress Cataloging-in-Publication Data

Green, Sara, 1964-
The Tennessee walking horse / by Sara Green.
    p. cm. – (Pilot books: horse breed roundup)
Includes bibliographical references and index.
 Summary: "Engaging images accompany information about the Tennessee Walking Horse. The combination of high-interest subject matter and narrative text is intended for students in grades 3 through 7"–Provided by publisher.
 ISBN 978-1-60014-660-2 (hardcover : alk. paper)
 1. Tennessee walking horse–Juvenile literature.  I. Title.
SF293.T4G74 2011
636.1'3–dc23                                    2011019076

Printed in the United States of America, North Mankato, MN.
080111        1187

# CONTENTS

# The Tennessee Walking Horse

You are riding a horse along a mountain path. Far below you, a sparkling river winds through a patch of evergreen trees. The trail is steep and uneven, but your ride is smooth and relaxing. You are on a Tennessee Walking Horse!

This breed, also known as the Walking horse, is world famous for its comfortable ride and gentle **temperament**. Walking horses make excellent family horses. They are easy to train and well suited for both beginning and experienced riders. Everyone enjoys the smooth **gait** of a Walking horse!

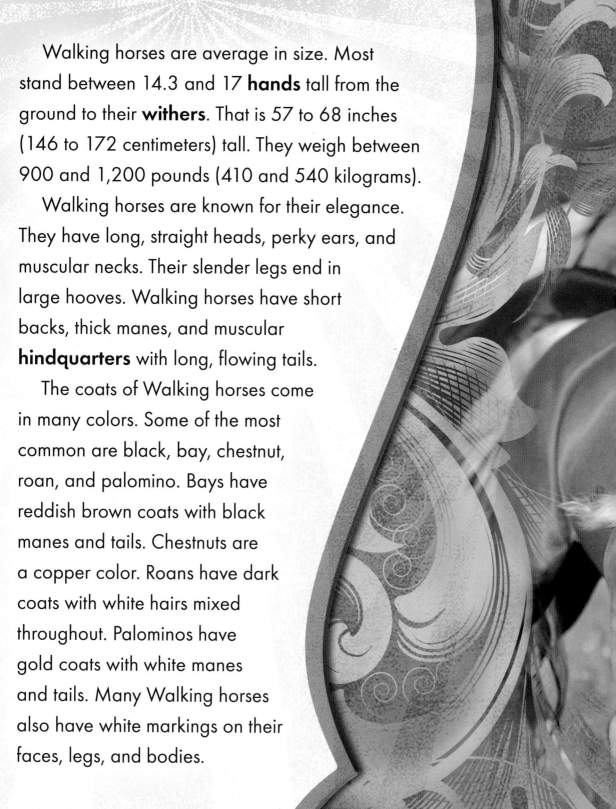

Walking horses are average in size. Most stand between 14.3 and 17 **hands** tall from the ground to their **withers**. That is 57 to 68 inches (146 to 172 centimeters) tall. They weigh between 900 and 1,200 pounds (410 and 540 kilograms).

Walking horses are known for their elegance. They have long, straight heads, perky ears, and muscular necks. Their slender legs end in large hooves. Walking horses have short backs, thick manes, and muscular **hindquarters** with long, flowing tails.

The coats of Walking horses come in many colors. Some of the most common are black, bay, chestnut, roan, and palomino. Bays have reddish brown coats with black manes and tails. Chestnuts are a copper color. Roans have dark coats with white hairs mixed throughout. Palominos have gold coats with white manes and tails. Many Walking horses also have white markings on their faces, legs, and bodies.

The gaits of Walking horses are different from other breeds. Walking horses have a large **overstride**, which is the secret to their smooth gait. A Walking horse's back feet step over the prints made by the front feet by as much as 18 inches (46 centimeters).

The **flat walk** is the Walking horse's slowest gait. The **running walk** is a faster version of the flat walk and is their most common gait. Their fastest gait is the **rocking chair canter**. It is named for its rocking motion. Walking horses can perform all three gaits for long periods of time without getting tired.

**Keep the Beat**
Walking horses often nod their heads and flick their ears in time with each step.

# Smooth Ride, Rough Terrain

The Walking horse breed began in the state of Tennessee. **Settlers** began arriving there in the 1800s to farm the land. They rode horses on their farms and used them to plow fields. The Tennessee ground was rocky and uneven. Farmers wanted horses that could give them a smooth ride over rough terrain for 40 to 50 miles (64 to 80 kilometers) every day. Farmers chose to **crossbreed** several horses. They used Saddlebreds for their smooth gaits, Morgans for their calm temperament, and Narragansett Pacers for their comfortable ride. They also included Thoroughbreds, Standardbreds, and Canadian Pacers for their **agility** and **endurance**. After many years of careful breeding, a **foal** named Black Allan was born in 1886. He was the first Tennessee Walking Horse.

## Walking Horse Celebration

One of the biggest national events for Walking horses and their breeders is the Tennessee Walking Horse National Celebration. The event is held in Shelbyville, Tennessee, which is nicknamed "The Walking Horse Capital of the World." Around 250,000 people attend this event every year to see which horse will be the World Grand Champion.

The Tennessee Walking Horse soon became popular all across the southern United States. Even when people started driving cars in the early 1900s, many still preferred to ride the smooth-gaited Walking horses on rough country roads.

In 1935, the Tennessee Walking Horse Breeders' and Exhibitors' Association (TWHBEA) formed. Its purpose was to **register** Walking horse foals. The Tennessee Walking Horse had become an official breed. The TWHBEA changed Black Allan's name to Allan F-1. The "F-1" identifies him as the breed's **foundation horse**. In order to be registered with the TWHBEA, foals must have two **purebred** parents. Today, over 500,000 Walking horses throughout the world are registered with the TWHBEA.

# Top Trail and Show Horses

If you love horseback riding on wilderness trails, the Walking horse is an ideal choice for you. With its calm temperament and smooth ride, the Walking horse will make your trail ride a comfortable, safe experience. You don't need to be a horse owner to enjoy a relaxing ride. Many trail riding businesses have Walking horses ready to hit the trail!

Walking horses are also used for **therapeutic riding**. These friendly horses help people with disabilities learn basic riding skills. Riders usually use the same horses every week so they can develop special bonds with their Walking horses.

## To Serve and Protect

Walking horses are popular park ranger and police horses. Their endurance allows them to walk over rough trails or city streets for hours without getting tired.

Walking horses do well on the trails, but they also excel in the **show ring**. Many riders and horses compete in the pleasure **class**. For this competition, riders have their horses perform gaits in front of judges. A judge announces the gaits one at a time, and riders direct their horses to perform them. Judges give points for the look of each gait and how well horses and riders work together. Horses often get extra points if they nod their heads in time with their steps!

There are two different pleasure classes. They are called English Pleasure and Western Pleasure. The two types have different commands, techniques, and rules. Each style also has its own **tack**. English riders sit on small saddles. They wear long boots and hats. Western riders sit on large saddles. They wear cowboy hats and western-style boots. Both English and Western class riders strive to show that their horses are a pleasure to ride.

**Don't Spill!**

The Water Glass Class is a competition in which riders show off the smooth gaits of their Tennessee Walking Horses. The riders enter an arena holding full glasses of water. The horses perform different gaits around the arena. At the end, the rider with the most water left wins!

Midnight Sun

# Famous Tennessee Walking Horses

## Wilson's Allen

Wilson's Allen was a chestnut Walking horse born in 1914 in Tennessee. He was a grandson of Black Allan. By the time he died in 1939, he had fathered 482 foals. Many of them grew up to be champion show horses. Wilson's Allen is buried near the Horse Science Center at Middle Tennessee University in Murfreesboro, Tennessee.

## Midnight Sun

Midnight Sun was a black Tennessee Walking Horse born in 1940. He was a foal of Wilson's Allen. In 1945 and 1946, Midnight Sun was named the World Grand Champion at the Tennessee Walking Horse National Celebration. A statue of Midnight Sun stands at the TWHBEA headquarters in Lewisburg, Tennessee.

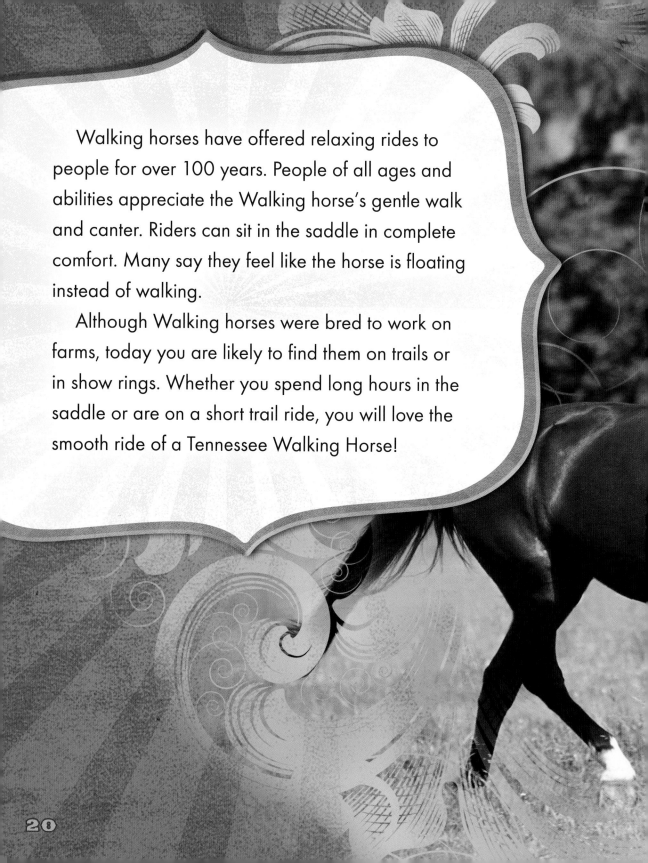

Walking horses have offered relaxing rides to people for over 100 years. People of all ages and abilities appreciate the Walking horse's gentle walk and canter. Riders can sit in the saddle in complete comfort. Many say they feel like the horse is floating instead of walking.

Although Walking horses were bred to work on farms, today you are likely to find them on trails or in show rings. Whether you spend long hours in the saddle or are on a short trail ride, you will love the smooth ride of a Tennessee Walking Horse!

# Glossary

**agility**—the ability to move the body quickly and with ease

**class**—a category of competition at a horse show

**crossbreed**—to use two different horse breeds to produce a new kind of horse

**endurance**—the ability to do something for a long time

**flat walk**—a relaxed walking pace in which a horse travels 4 to 8 miles (6 to 13 kilometers) per hour; the flat walk is one of the gaits of the Tennessee Walking Horse.

**foal**—a young horse; foals are under one year old.

**foundation horse**—one of the first horses of a specific breed; all horses of a breed can trace their bloodlines back to foundation horses.

**gait**—the way in which a horse moves; walking, trotting, and cantering are examples of gaits.

**hands**—the units used to measure the height of a horse; one hand is equal to 4 inches (10.2 centimeters).

**hindquarters**—the hind legs and muscles of a four-legged animal

**overstride**—when a horse's back hooves come down ahead of the prints of its front hooves

**purebred**—born from parents of the same breed

**register**—to make record of; owners register their horses with official breed organizations.

**rocking chair canter**—a smooth run with a swinging motion; the rocking chair canter is one of the gaits of the Tennessee Walking Horse.

**running walk**—a smooth gait in which a horse travels 10 to 20 miles (16 to 32 kilometers) per hour; the running walk is one of the gaits of the Tennessee Walking horse.

**settlers**—people who come to live in a new land

**show ring**—the ring in which horses compete and are displayed at a horse show

**tack**—any equipment used to ride a horse

**temperament**—personality or nature; the Tennessee Walking Horse has a gentle, calm temperament.

**therapeutic riding**—horseback riding for people with disabilities; therapeutic riding helps improve their balance, strength, and self-confidence.

**withers**—the ridge between the shoulder blades of a horse

# To Learn More

## At the Library

Coleman, Lori. *The Tennessee Walking Horse*. Mankato, Minn.: Capstone Press, 2006.

Felder, Deborah G. *Changing Times: The Story of a Tennessee Walking Horse and the Girl Who Proves That Grown-Ups Don't Always Know Best*. Dyersville, Iowa: Ertl Co., 1996.

Wilcox, Charlotte. *The Tennessee Walking Horse*. Mankato, Minn.: Capstone Press, 1996.

## On the Web

Learning more about
Tennessee Walking Horses is as easy as 1, 2, 3.

1. Go to www.factsurfer.com.

2. Enter "Tennessee Walking Horses" into the search box.

3. Click the "Surf" button and you will see a list of related Web sites.

With factsurfer.com, finding more information
is just a click away.

# Index

The images in this book are reproduced through the courtesy of: Juniors Bildarchiv, front cover; Sabine Stuewer / KimballStock, pp. 4-5; Wildlife GmbH / Alamy, pp. 6-7; Juniors Bildarchiv / Alamy, pp. 8-9, 18-19, 20-21; Only Horses Tbk / Alamy, pp. 10-11, 12; Associated Press, pp. 14-15; Sarah K. Andrew, pp. 16-17; Public Domain, p. 18 (small).